WELCOME TO
GRAND TETON NATIONAL PARK

⛺

CONTENTS

A Slice of the Wild West

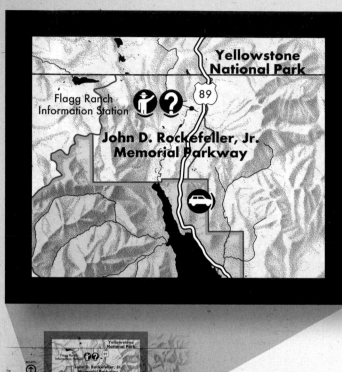

Yellowstone National Park

Flagg Ranch Information Station

John D. Rockefeller, Jr. Memorial Parkway

Welcome to Grand Teton National Park! You're in the western state of Wyoming. Look at those beautiful mountains! The Tetons are the youngest and most rugged peaks in the Rocky Mountains.

Grand Teton National Park sits in the largest patch of wild lands in America, outside of Alaska. This area is known as the Greater Yellowstone **Ecosystem**. This natural community is about the size of West Virginia. This area includes Grand Teton and Yellowstone National Parks, three national wildlife refuges, and six national forests and **wilderness areas**. The animals move from one area to another. So do visitors. The two national parks are connected by the John D. Rockefeller, Jr. Memorial Parkway.

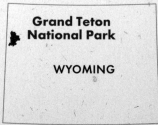

Grand Teton National Park

WYOMING

WELCOME TO
GRAND TETON
NATIONAL PARK

BY MARIBETH LORBIECKI

Content Consultant: Jackie Skaggs, Public Affairs Specialist, Grand Teton National Park

MAP KEY
The maps throughout this
book use the following icons:

 Bear Viewing Area

 Campground

Driving Excursion

Elk Viewing Area

Hiking Trail

Lodging

Marmot Viewing Area

Point of Interest

Ranger Station

 Visitor Center

Wildflower Area

Wooded Area

About National Parks

A national park is an area of land that has been set aside by Congress. National parks protect nature and history. In most cases, no hunting, grazing, or farming is allowed. The first national park in the United States—and in the world—was Yellowstone National Park. It is located in parts of Wyoming, Idaho, and Montana. It was founded in 1872. In 1916, the U.S. National Park Service began.

Today, the National Park Service manages more than 380 sites. Some of these sites are historic, such as the Statue of Liberty or Martin Luther King, Jr. National Historic Site. Other park areas preserve wild land. The National Park Service manages 40% of the nation's wilderness areas, including national parks. Each year, millions of people from around the world visit these national parks. Visitors may camp, go canoeing, or go for a hike. Or, they may simply sit and enjoy the scenery, wildlife, and the quiet of the land.

TABLE OF

The Child's World®

Published in the United States of America by The Child's World®

PO Box 326
Chanhassen, MN 55317-0326
800-599-READ
www.childsworld.com

Acknowledgements
The Child's World®: Mary Berendes, Publishing Director

The Design Lab: Kathleen Petelinsek, Design and Page Production

Map Hero, Inc.: Matt Kania, Cartographer

Red Line Editorial: Bob Temple, Editorial Direction

Photo Credits
Cover and this page: Bill Ross/Corbis

Interior: Blake Woken/Corbis: 7; Chase Swift/Corbis: 13; Collection of the Jackson Hole Historical Society and Museum: 17; Gunter Marx Photography/Corbis: 9; Kennan Ward/Corbis: 11, 21; Kevin R. Morris/Corbis: 16, 19; Lester Lefkowitz/Corbis: 12; Marc Muench/Corbis: 23; Pat O'Hara/Corbis: 14–15; Ric Ergenbright/Corbis: 18; Richard Hamilton Smith/Corbis: 24–25; Robert Y. Ono/Corbis: 1, 26; Ron Watts/Corbis: 2–3

Library of Congress Cataloging-in-Publication Data
Lorbiecki, Marybeth.
  Welcome to Grand Teton National Park / by Marybeth Lorbiecki.
    p. cm. — (Visitor guides)
  Includes index.
  ISBN 1-59296-698-5 (library bound : alk. paper)
  1. Grand Teton National Park (Wyo.)—Juvenile literature. I. Title. II. Series.
  F767.T3L67 2006
  917.87'55—dc22   2005030073

On the cover and this page
Even at night, Grand Teton National Park is one of the most beautiful places on Earth.

On page 1
Grand Teton is the tallest peak in the park. At 13,770 feet (4,197 m), the peak is sometimes covered by wispy clouds.

On pages 2–3
The views along the Snake River are some of the most beautiful in the park.

The Teton Park Road runs along the base of the Tetons. It offers close-up views of the mountains and scenic stops where you can take a photograph or look for wildlife.

Walk on the Wild Side

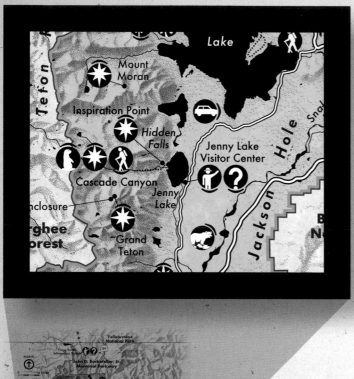

Head to Jenny Lake Visitor Center, and see the sparkling blue-green water of glacial Jenny Lake. Thousands of years ago, large sheets of moving ice called **glaciers** carved the **canyons** of the Teton Mountains. When the ice melted, lakes were left on the valley floor. The glistening blue water is especially clear. Jenny Lake is too cold and too deep for water plants to grow.

At the dock, a shuttle boat awaits you for a trip to Hidden Falls. Climb aboard! A park tour guide will give you an introduction to this amazing place. Once you've crossed the lake, prepare to hike. The trail winds its way to the falls. If you've packed water and snacks, go all the way to Inspiration Point. From there, you can look down across the valley below. If you are really adventurous, keep hiking. Stop and have lunch along the way. You'll get a view of the stunning **Cascade** Canyon. Keep your eyes alert! You may see a pika, a yellow-bellied marmot, or even a moose.

Reminders of the Ice Age

Some signs of the last Ice Age can still be seen. Look at the snowy areas that decorate the park's peaks. The snow is there even in the summer. Many of these areas are glaciers. They melt and freeze at a slow rate.

Jenny Lake is the second largest lake in the park (the largest lake is Jackson Lake). The lake sits at the base of Grand Teton, and visitors often rent boats to use on the calm waters. You can get some of the best pictures of the peak from the middle of the lake.

A Hike to Alaska

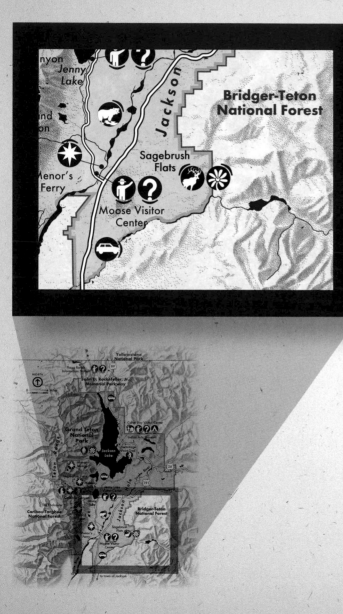

Bridger-Teton National Forest

Sagebrush Flats

Menor's Ferry

Moose Visitor Center

When you hike in the Tetons, many trails go from the valley to a peak. It's like climbing from Colorado to Alaska. You go through five different nature communities that are based on weather, soil, and water. They are sagebrush **flats**, wet meadows, rivers and lakes, spruce and pine forests, and **alpine** meadows. Each area is a small ecosystem, and in each one you'll see different plants and wildlife.

You'll find sagebrush flats on the dry valley floor. Sage, grasses, and wildflowers carpet the ground. You may see bison, pronghorn antelope, ground squirrels, coyotes, and badgers. Sage grouse, meadowlarks, and red-tailed hawks can also be seen. If you're lucky, you may even spot a wolf.

🚶🚶 A lone bison grazes in a meadow near Grand Teton. This picture shows some of the different nature communities found in the park. The bison is grazing on the sagebrush flats. Behind the bison, you can see a forest. Another forest grows farther in the distance, stopping about halfway up the mountain.

The Snake River flows through the southern part of Yellowstone National Park before entering Grand Teton National Park. The river enters Jackson Lake, passes through Jackson Lake Dam, and then winds its way slowly through the rest of the park.

In some areas along the trail are low spots where water gathers. These are the wet meadows. Willows provide shade. Plenty of small animals such as water-loving snakes, frogs, lizards, and salamanders dart, hop, swim, and slither here. Moose gorge on willows and water plants.

The park's rivers, lakes, and marshes offer homes to many creatures. Birds warble around gleaming glacial lakes. Ducks land noisily on marshes. Trout glide along in the Snake River as otters pounce and play. Eagles soar overhead, and osprey dive. Visitors can raft, canoe, and swim.

Look toward the skyline along towering lodgepole pine, fir, and spruce. These are the high forests. Trees in these cool forests clean the air. They give off a fresh, pungent scent. Elk munch on grass, while mule deer feast on tree bark and seedlings. Black bear waddle around in search of roots, berries, and bugs.

Stay Back from Animals

The animals in the park might seem tame, but they are not. Give wildlife a lot of space, or they get frightened. Don't ever come up to a wild animal, not even for a photo. Leave at least 50 yards (46 m) between you. Stay away from their young, too. Wild animals don't like humans going near their babies.

Bear Safety

Here are some tips to help you stay safe in bear country.

- Make noise. Sing, whistle, or talk as you hike. If bears know you're nearby, they will avoid you!
- Be alert. If you see fresh tracks, hike somewhere else.
- Stay far away. If you spot a bear, give it lots of space.
- Store all food in air-tight containers. Never keep food in your tent!

Up in the highest lands, beyond most trees, you will see more rock and less soil. These are the alpine meadows and **tundra**. Be careful to stay on the trail, because the plants up here are fragile. Lichens cover the rocks. The few trees in this area are small and twisted. Many of them are hundreds of years old. Wildflowers display their vivid colors. Bighorn sheep ramble. Cold winds whistle and snow is never far away. In these wildest and harshest areas, grizzly bears roam freely. They can move to other parts of the park as well. Bears like this area because they are usually left alone.

Like other higher areas in the Tetons, this mountain meadow is carpeted with wildflowers. Here you can see yellow alpine sunflowers, pink sticky geraniums, blue lupines, and white yarrow.

Native Americans began using the valley known as Jackson Hole 11,000 years ago. They lived and hunted in the area, as well as held religious ceremonies. Jackson Hole was named for David Jackson, an 1800s fur trader who was one of the founders of the Rocky Mountain Fur Company.

Down to Jackson Hole

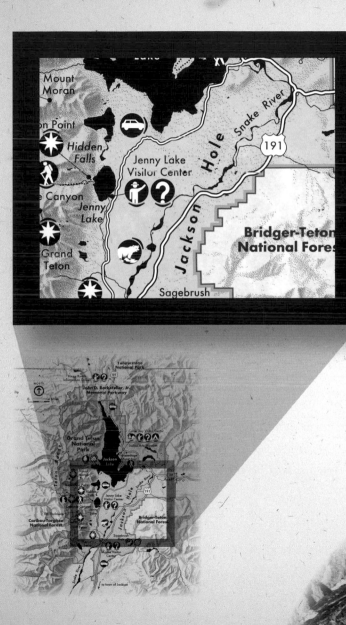

Fur trappers named any valley surrounded by mountains or cliffs a "hole." Jackson Hole was a favorite place for native peoples. Here they hunted animals and gathered plants. Jackson Hole remains a beloved place for the Shoshone and other nations. These mountains have long been a place for them to make "vision quests." They pray and seek guidance about their life and their people. On the summit of Grand Teton, a number of rocks stand upright in a circle. This area, pictured below, is called, "The Enclosure." It is thought to be especially significant. Some native spiritual leaders believe the Tetons are the hub of a Medicine Wheel of holy sites across America.

Hole Up in Jackson

The nearby town of Jackson is full of Old West history. Clomp down the wooden sidewalks. Watch the nightly gun fight, or hoot and holler at the rodeo. Go ahead and experience some of the other fun things to do in this Wild West town.

The valley was named Jackson's Hole after David E. Jackson. He was a fur trader who trapped animals for their fur here in 1829. Eventually, the name was shortened. Ranchers began to follow the fur traders. The ranchers brought cattle. At Menor's Ferry, you can still see a general store, an old cabin, and the rebuilt ferryboat of homesteader Bill Menor. He lived here in the 1890s and early 1900s.

Bill Menor was one of the first settlers in the Jackson Hole area. Soon after arriving in 1892, Menor built several buildings along the Snake River. He then built a ferry (a flat raft) that carried people, goods, and horses across the river. The settlement of Menor's Ferry is near the present-day village of Moose, Wyoming.

A Long View through History

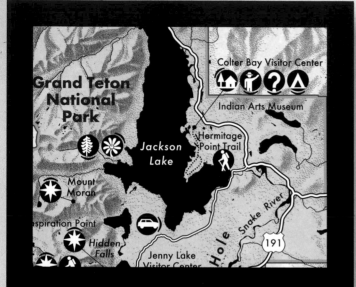

Grand Teton National Park

Colter Bay Visitor Center

Indian Arts Museum

Hermitage Point Trail

Jackson Lake

Mount Moran

spiration Point

Hidden Falls

Jenny Lake Visitor Center

Hole Snake River

191

The Old West isn't really very old around here! For a look back in time, go to Colter Bay. Take a hike on the Hermitage Point Trail. Choose the left fork that turns for Swan Lake. This scenic trail will bring you around the lake. Climb a small hill, and you'll get a terrific view of Mount Moran.

Staring at Mount Moran and Swan Lake, you can imagine the extreme history of this land. Not far from your feet lies an earthquake **fault**. This crack in the **Earth's crust** runs along the base of the Tetons. Millions of years ago, earthquakes shifted the land along this fault line. Mountains of **granite** and **gneiss** rose into the sky. The valley was created. Then came a long period in which the land was covered by glaciers. They melted, and wild plants sprouted. Soon, animals arrived. Finally, people came!

Indian Life

On your way back to the modern age, stop at the Colter Bay Visitor Center and Indian Arts Museum. You'll learn so much more about the park and its history. See objects made and used by the many Native Americans who once lived here.

Mount Moran seems to sparkle as the sun begins to rise. The mountain isn't as tall as Grand Teton, but at 12,605 feet (3,842 m), it's still very impressive. Mount Moran is named for Thomas Moran, who was a famous landscape artist in the late 1800s.

Adventurous Science

Jackson Lake

Hermitage Point Trail

Mount Moran

Point

Hidden Falls

Canyon

Jenny Lake

Jenny Lake Visitor Center

Grand

Jackson Hole

Snake River

191

Bridger-Teton National Forest

If you don't have a snow parka, the best months to visit are July and August. It's sunny, warm, and jam-packed with things to do. Watch the wildlife. Take a raft trip on the Snake River. Go horseback riding. Enjoy a long hike, perhaps even a stargazing walk at night. Go canoeing, fishing, backpacking, or rock climbing. Then be sure to rest your feet by a crackling fire. Stare up into a night bursting with stars.

The Exum Ridge is a favorite place for mountain climbers to test their skills. The Ridge is divided into two parts: the upper and the lower. These two climbers are making their way over rocks on the upper Exum Ridge area.

May, September, and October are usually still warm enough to enjoy the area. In winter, activities change. Snowshoeing, cross-country skiing, snowmobiling, and ice fishing are all options at this time of year. And that's just the beginning.

Don't miss the Young Naturalist program. If you are here for a long visit, check out the Teton Science School. That's where kids work with scientists to study this great "land" laboratory—the Greater Yellowstone Ecosystem. There are week-long programs for students in third through eighth grades. There are also family and teacher workshops. Programs for high-school and college students are available, too. Everyone gets a chance to study nature in the wild outdoors.

The Science Laboratories

Research is always going on in the Greater Yellowstone Ecosystem. Some subjects being studied now include the migration path of the pronghorn antelope, diseases in bison, how fire affects the wild plant and animal communities, and the ways of the wolverines, wolves, and grizzlies.

Enjoy incredible views along the snowmobile trail, which runs from Moran Junction to Flagg Ranch, near Yellowstone's south entrance.

"The Old Patriarch" is another one of the park's treasures. This very old limber pine tree was struck by lightning many years ago. The strike seared off part of the tree's main branches, leaving it with its gnarly look. The Old Patriarch and its meadow is one of the most photographed spots in the park.

The Gift of a Park

Having now explored this place, you can understand why it is so treasured. John D. Rockefeller, Jr. loved the Teton country, too. He bought and donated more than 33,000 acres (13,355 hectares) to the park. This gift expanded the original Grand Teton Park. The 24,000-acre (9,712-hectare) John D. Rockefeller, Jr. Memorial Parkway links Grand Teton and Yellowstone national parks and was named in his honor.

Now it's up to all of us to take care of this park. It's our job to preserve its ecosystems. Then we can pass it on as gift to everyone who comes after us.

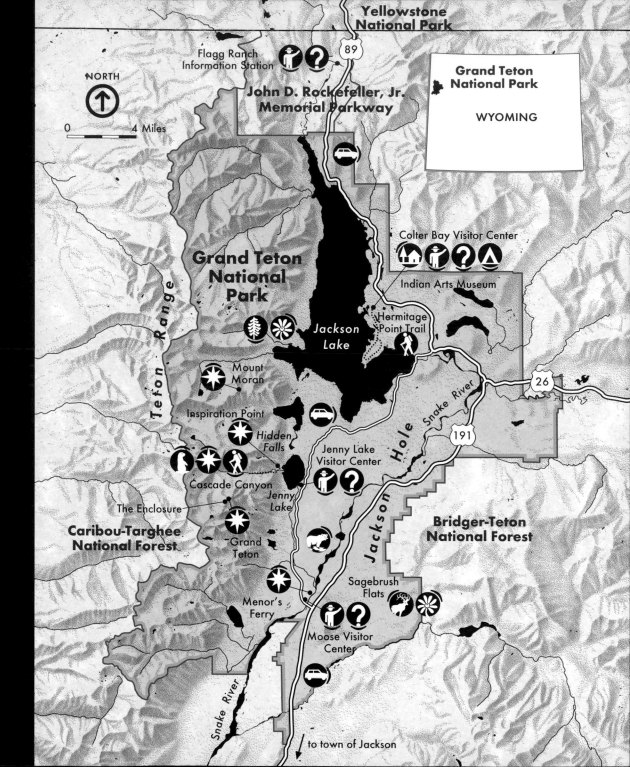

Yellowstone
National Park

Flagg Ranch
Information Station

89

NORTH

0   4 Miles

John D. Rockefeller, Jr.
Memorial Parkway

Grand Teton
National Park

WYOMING

Colter Bay Visitor Center

Indian Arts Museum

Grand Teton
National
Park

Jackson
Lake

Hermitage
Point Trail

Teton Range

Mount
Moran

Inspiration Point

Hidden
Falls

Jenny Lake
Visitor Center

26

191

Jackson Hole Snake River

Cascade Canyon

Jenny
Lake

The Enclosure

Caribou-Targhee
National Forest

Grand
Teton

Bridger-Teton
National Forest

Menor's
Ferry

Sagebrush
Flats

Moose Visitor
Center

Snake River

to town of Jackson

GRAND TETON NATIONAL PARK FAST FACTS

Date founded: Original park, 1929; expanded in 1950

Location: Western Wyoming

Size: 485 square miles/1,256 sq km; 310,400 acres/125,614 hectares

Major habitats: Sagebrush flats, wet meadows, rivers and lakes, spruce and pine forests, and alpine meadows

Important landforms: Peaks, glaciers, Snake River, Jackson Lake

Elevation:
   Highest: 13,770 feet/4,197 m (Grand Teton)
   Lowest: 6,350 feet/1,935 m (park's south boundary)

Weather:
   Average yearly rainfall: 10 inches/25 cm
   Average yearly snowfall: 191 inches/485 cm
   Hottest temperature: 93 F/34 C
   Coolest temperature: -46 F/-43 C

Number of animal species: 17 species of carnivores, 6 species of hoofed animals, 22 species of rodents, 16 species of fish, 4 species of reptiles, and more than 300 species of birds

Number of plant species: 7 species of conifer trees and more than 900 species of flowering plants

Number of endangered or threatened animal species: 5

Native people: Shoshone, Gros Ventre, Flathead, Blackfoot, Crow, and Nez Perce

Number of visitors each year: 3.5 to 4 million

Important sites and landmarks: Major peaks, the Snake River and its tributaries, seven glacial lakes, 200 miles (322 km) of hiking trails, historic Menor's Ferry, pioneer/ranch buildings, Indian Arts Museum, Jackson Lake Dam, and 252 miles (406 km) of hiking trails

Tourist activities: Wildlife watching in five different natural communities, climbing, rafting, canoeing, fishing, horseback riding, and photography

GLOSSARY

alpine (AL-pine): An area of land so high that it is above the place where trees grow easily is called alpine. The alpine areas in Grand Teton National Park have only a few wind-twisted trees because it is too cold and dry for most trees.

canyons (KAN-yunz): Deep, narrow valleys surrounded by cliffs are called canyons. Grand Teton National Park has several canyons.

cascade (kass-KAYD): A steep, rushing fall of water that drops from level to level is called a cascade. Grand Teton National Park has a trail that leads to a canyon with a cascading waterfall in it.

Earth's crust (ERTHS KRUST): The thick layer of hardened rock covering the inner core of the planet is called the Earth's crust. A crack in this crust lies under the park, and it caused the earthquakes that pushed up the peaks.

ecosystem (EE-koh-sis-tum): A community of plants and animals that depend on each other and share the same weather and water systems is an ecosystem. Grand Teton National Park has five different ecosytems.

fault (FALT): A crack in the crust of the planet is called a fault. The earthquakes that happened thousands of years ago in the park happened along a fault line.

flats (FLATS): The plains, or low, flat spots of the valley floor, are called flats. The flats in Grand Teton National Park are known for the sagebrush growing in them.

glaciers (GLAY-shurz): Huge masses of slow-moving ice are glaciers. The peaks in Grand Teton National Park have glaciers on them.

gneiss (NICE): Gneiss is a very hard rock that is mixed and melted like granite but also contains crushed bits of long-dead plants and animals. Grand Teton's peaks also have gneiss in them.

granite (GRAN-it): Granite is a very hard rock formed of crystals (such as quartz) and minerals molten together in the hot areas of the Earth's core. Grand Teton's peaks have granite in them.

tundra (TUN-dra): A treeless area of fragile, frozen or half-frozen soil is a tundra. As in other tundras, the tundra in the park is covered by lichen, mosses, and dwarfed shrubs.

wilderness areas (WIL-der-ness AYR-ee-uz): A large area of wild, natural land without human-made buildings and roads is called a wilderness area. There are three areas protected as wilderness around Grand Teton National Park: Vinegar Hole Wilderness, Jedediah Smith Wilderness, and the Teton Wilderness.

TO FIND OUT MORE

FURTHER READING

Craighead, Shirley A.
*Bugling Elk and Sleeping Grizzlies: The Who, What, and
When of Yellowstone and Grand Teton National Parks.*
Guilford, CT: Falcon, 2004.

Holdsworth, Henry.
Born Wild in Yellowstone and Grand Teton National Parks.
Helena, MT: Farcountry Press, 2003.

Petersen, David.
Grand Teton National Park.
Chicago: Children's Press, 1992.

Salts, Bobbi.
Discover Grand Teton National Park: An Educational Activity Book for Kids.
Moose, WY: Grand Teton Natural History Association, 1992.

ON THE WEB

Visit our home page for lots of links
about Grand Teton National Park:

http://www.childsworld.com/links

NOTE TO PARENTS, TEACHERS, AND LIBRARIANS:
We routinely check our Web links to make sure
they're safe, active sites—so encourage your
readers to check them out!

🚶 ABOUT THE AUTHOR

Marybeth Lorbiecki has written over twenty books, most of them award-winners. She loves to bring history alive for readers, and has written books on such fascinating people as Jackie Robinson, Martin Luther King, Jr., and John Muir. Lorbiecki also loves to write about nature and wildlife, covering such subjects as Earth care and prairie dogs. In *Welcome to Grand Teton National Park,* Lorbiecki combines her love for history and nature in an exploration of this incredible national treasure. Lorbiecki lives in Hudson, Wisconsin, with her husband, David Mataya, and their three children, Nadja, Mirjana, and Dmitri.

INDEX